DATE DUE

Savannas
Life in the Tropical Grasslands

Savannas
Life in the Tropical Grasslands

Laurie Peach Toupin

Franklin Watts
A Division of Scholastic Inc.
New York • Toronto • London • Auckland • Sydney
Mexico City • New Delhi • Hong Kong
Danbury, Connecticut

To our daughter, Maria:
May you visit these wonderful grasslands someday.

Note to readers: Definitions for words in **bold** can be found in the Glossary at the back of this book.

Photographs © 2005: Animals Animals: 40 bottom (Michael Fogden), 32, 40 top (Gerald Hinde/ABPL), 25 (Joe McDonald); Corbis Images: 2 (Ralph A. Clevenger), 20 right (D. Robert & Lorri Franz), 11 (Martin Harvey), 35 (Tom Van Sant), 20 left (Jim Zuckerman); Earth Scenes: 18 (Breck P. Kent), cover (S. Osolinski/OSF); Minden Pictures: 5 left, 22 (Tui De Roy), 27 (Mitsuhiko Imamori), 30 (Mitsuaki Iwago), 21 (Mark Moffett), 5 right, 28 (Yva Momatiuk), 14 (Shin Yoshino); NHPA: 44 (Martin Harvey), 24 (Image Quest 3-D), 19 (Andy Rouse), 10 (Dave Watts); Peter Arnold Inc.: 51 (BIOS), 50 (William Campbell), 36 (M & C Denis-Huot), 9 (Mark Edwards), 6, 31 (Martin Harvey), 46 (Frank Kroenke), 43 (Luiz C. Marigo); Photo Researchers, NY: 34 (Francois Gohier), 39 (Mark Newman); Courtesy of Scott Turner: 26; Visuals Unlimited/Cabisco: 12.

Illustration p. 17 by Bob Italiano

The photograph on the cover shows a savanna in Kenya. The photograph opposite the title page shows a herd of African elephants.

Library of Congress Cataloging-in-Publication Data

Toupin, Laurie Peach.
    Savannas : life in the tropical grasslands / Laurie Peach Toupin.— 1st ed.
       p. cm. — (Biomes and habitats)
    Includes bibliographical references (p.   ).
    ISBN 0-531-12386-3 (lib. bdg.)
    1. Savanna ecology—Juvenile literature. I. Title. II. Series.
QH541.5.P7T682 2005
577.4'8—dc22
                                     2004013281

Contents

Lions and topi, a type of antelope, dwell side by side on the African Savanna. The topi are safe at the moment, as lions typically hunt at night.

Chapter One

Too Dry, Too Wet . . . Ah, Home!

Sam McNaughton and his friend walked down to the Seronera River on the Serengeti Plain to check out the fencing for a research project involving tree growth along streams. As this was McNaughton's first time researching the Serengeti, the Syracuse University biology professor didn't think twice about leaving the Land Rover some 300 yards

(273 meters) away. He didn't feel the same way when he turned around and saw eight snarling lions lying down across from their truck.

McNaughton cautiously walked to position the Land Rover between himself and the animals. "As we got closer, a couple of the lions left, but the rest began to snarl even more," he says. "I thought that this was the end of my Serengeti research." When the men were safely within reach of the vehicle, they sprinted. "We made it, but I was much more careful about how far away I left my Land Rover after that!"

Such is the life on the African tropical grassland—perhaps the most famous savanna in the world. African tropical grasslands and their inhabitants have been the backdrop of countless movies, television shows, books, and plays, such as *Tarzan* and *Out of Africa*. Some of the fastest, largest, and most ferocious land creatures on the planet live here. The grassland covers more than one-third of the African continent.

Not the Only One

The terms *tropical grassland* and *savanna* are interchangeable. There are other tropical grasslands in the world as well— places where high temperatures and grasses dominate.

South America has two such areas: the llanos north of the Amazon Rain Forest and the campos south of it.

Llano is from the Spanish word for "plain." The Orinoco River flows along the southern edge of this 220,000-square-mile (570,000-square-kilometer) grassy area. Every year

during the rainy season, the river and its tributaries flood the plains, replenishing the land with rich soil. When the area isn't flooded, it is affected by drought. Even so, an incredible amount of wildlife and five million cattle, horses, and donkeys call it home.

The **campo**, which means "open pasture" in Portuguese, is made up of two distinct savannas in Brazil. The *campo cerrado*, meaning closed field, is partly forested. Few trees grow on the *campo sujo*, which means "dirty field." The campos make up almost one-fourth of the country. More than ten thousand different plant species grow here, making the campos second only to the tropical rain forest in plant **diversity**, the number

The Orinoco River is one of the five largest river systems in South America and lies entirely within Venezuela.

9

Kangaroos belong to a small group of animals called macropods, which means "big foot." With such big feet, the Eastern grey kangaroo can jump 30 feet (9 m) in one hop.

of different species living in a given area. Many of these plants are used as sources of medicine.

Tropical grasslands in Australia are home to **marsupials**, or animals that carry their young in a pocket, such as kangaroos, wallabies, and wombats.

Grasslands in India and Southeast Asia are considered a kind of artificial savanna that was created when forests were burned or cut down to clear the land for farming.

Precious Resource

Three factors formed these large expanses of grassland: climate, soil, and fire. Life in tropical grasslands revolves around rain. Eating, sleeping, mating, and giving birth all revolve around precipitation. Even the seasons are determined by rainfall instead of temperature, and there are only two: the rainy season and the dry season.

The rainy season can last between seven and nine months. During this time, the majority of the year's rain falls. The dry season really is dry. In Australia, for instance, up to 94 inches (240 centimeters) of rain can fall during the rainy season, which lasts from September to April. Yet in the dry season (May to August), there is often no precipitation for two or three months in a row. Trees and other woody vegetation have a hard time surviving in such conditions.

These seasonal periods are still called summer and winter.

Temperatures in the summer can climb above 90 degrees Fahrenheit (32 degrees Celsius), while the temperature on the coldest day in the winter may fall to 64 degrees F (18 degrees C).

Rainy seasons and dry seasons are caused by the movement of the **Intertropical Convergence Zone**. This zone is located around Earth near the equator, where the trade winds of the northern and southern hemispheres meet. The intense sun and warm water of the equator heat the air in the zone, increasing its humidity and causing the air to rise. As the air rises, it cools and releases the moisture in the form of thunderstorms.

When the Intertropical Convergence Zone is directly over a region, rainfall is heavy. When it isn't, the area may receive no rain. Long-term changes in the location of the zone can result in severe droughts or flooding.

Elephants must bathe to keep cool and their skin free from parasites and diseases. If water cannot be found, elephants will sometimes use regurgitated water from their stomachs.

During the dry season, green grasslands turn into barren wastelands.

Digging Deeper

Some tropical grasslands receive enough rain to sustain trees, yet only grasses grow. In these areas, one has to look below the surface of the ground to find out why. Soil conditions have to be just right for tree growth. The treeless nature of the south-eastern Serengeti Plain in Africa is the result of an **impermeable** crust of clay that sits about 40 inches (1 m) below the surface. This crust prevents plants with deep roots, like trees, from growing.

A Little Spark

Fire is probably the single most important element in keeping the tropical grasslands free of trees. Tropical grasslands explode into flames almost every year. Natural fires usually occur right before the rainy season starts, when grass is dry and thick clouds bring lightning but no rain. One fire may rage over the grassland for days or weeks before the first rain falls. Some animals actually use these blazes to their advantage. The black kite, or fire hawk, lives in Africa and India. This bird often hunts along the edge of the fire for animals fleeing the flames.

These fires help the grassland in two important ways. First, they prevent woody plants from taking root. Second, they help replenish the soil with nutrients. **Litter**, or dead leaves, stems, and flowers, contains valuable nutrients needed for new plants to grow. Fire decomposes the litter instantly, allowing the nutrients stored in it to return to the soil in the form of ash. This gives plants and grasses access to these nutrients more quickly than if they had waited for the litter to decay.

People have suppressed fires over the years. In Australia, wildfires were actively smothered because they were thought to be dangerous. Fire suppression not only allows large numbers of trees and shrubs to grow, but also prevents the soil from being replenished with nutrients. Today, biologists work with landowners to develop **controlled burn** practices. In a controlled burn, people purposely set and manage a fire, confining it to a certain area of land.

Climate, soil, and fire have so dramatically influenced the wildlife found on tropical grasslands that many species are found nowhere else. This type of natural community, formed by climatic and environmental conditions, is called a **biome**. This book takes a look at the tropical grassland biome and those organisms that call it home.

Dirty Name

Edaphic savannas are grasslands that are created by soil conditions. Edaphic refers to soil as it affects living organisms.

The Masai Mara National Reserve in Kenya, where *Out of Africa* was filmed, is one of the most well-known and popular wildlife preserves in Africa.

Chapter Two

Grasses Rule

In tropical grasslands, grasses rule. All forms of wildlife and vegetation depend on them for survival. But to rule here, one has to be tough. Grasses can be eaten, trampled, flooded, dried out, and burned without dying. In fact, tropical grasses thrive in these harsh conditions. Everything about a grass plant makes it the perfect savanna inhabitant: its root system, leaf shape, and method of growing.

Long Roots

Grasses are hollow-stemmed plants with narrow leaves and extensive root systems.

A Complex Balance

Nothing would survive on the savanna without the grasses and other flowering plants—the **producers** of the biome. Plants produce their own food. Chlorophyll allows them to capture energy from sunlight through a process called **photosynthesis**. During photosynthesis, green plants use sunlight to change the hydrogen from water (H_2O) and the carbon and oxygen from carbon dioxide (CO_2) into sugar. The plant then releases oxygen as waste. The plant uses this sugar, along with minerals from the soil to produce the substances it needs to survive.

Animals that eat the plants are called **herbivores**. Those that eat both producers and herbivores are called **omnivores**. Animals that feed on herbivores and omnivores are called **carnivores**. When everything dies, **decomposers**, such as fungi and bacteria, break down the remains, returning precious nutrients to the soil for use by plants. All together, these living organisms make up a food web.

Roots make up more than nine-tenths of the grass plant. Elephant grasses, for example, may grow to be more than 10 feet (3 m) tall, but their roots stretch at least that far below the surface. You would find it difficult to pull out savanna grasses like you could those in your school's field.

The root systems of savanna grasses absorb water and minerals from the soil and store food. Although the above-ground portion of a grass plant may be destroyed by drought, for example, savanna grasses survive because enough energy is stored in the root network to produce new growth.

A Functional Shape

In tropical rain forests, where there is plenty of rain, ground plants have broad leaves. Water is not an issue. Instead, the plants have to compete for the sunlight that filters through the leaves of tall trees. In tropical grasslands, however, plants receive sufficient light to grow because there are few trees to block the sun. Instead, they need to conserve water.

The narrow shape of the grass leaf helps keep the plant alive during the long dry season because it has such a small surface area for **transpiration**—the process through which water evaporates from a leaf. The narrower the leaf, the less water is lost. Some plants will even fold over or close upon themselves to prevent water loss.

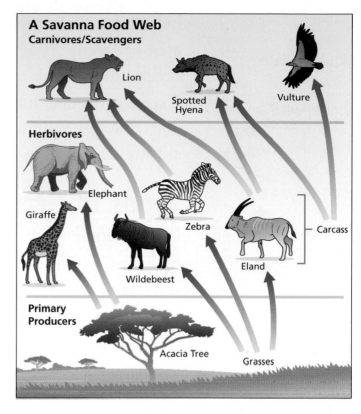

A Savanna Food Web
Carnivores/Scavengers
Lion
Spotted Hyena
Vulture
Herbivores
Elephant
Giraffe
Zebra
Eland
Carcass
Wildebeest
Primary Producers
Acacia Tree
Grasses

Fireproof

Right at ground level, where the stem and roots meet, sits the **basal meristem**—the growing point of the grass plant. Even though fire may destroy the leaves, the grass's growing point remains unaffected, and the plant will simply grow back. In contrast, a tree's growing points are located at the tips of the branches. Some trees die when these spots are burned.

A Little Help from Below

Another reason grass is so hardy is that it gets a little help from microorganisms that dwell in the soil. **Cyanobacteria** are one such example. These bacteria add nitrogen to the soil—a necessary nutrient for plants—by fixing or pulling nitrogen gas from the air. They then turn the gas into ammonia (NH_3), nitrites (NO_2), or nitrates (NO_3), which can be absorbed by plants and used to produce food.

Savanna soil also contains an **enzyme** called urease that

Vulnerable Grasses

Grasses, like animals, are affected by environmental changes. Biologists estimate that many grass species are extinct, endangered, or threatened.

There are several types of savannas, named according to the plants that grow there. This acacia savanna is a mixture of grass and acacia trees.

helps replenish nitrogen. An enzyme is a substance that creates, or speeds up, a chemical reaction. This enzyme instantly breaks down a substance found in animal urine called urea. Urease turns urea into ammonium. Because ammonium contains nitrogen and hydrogen, the nitrogen component is available to plants within minutes of an animal urinating.

Types of Grass

Grasses come in all shapes and sizes. There are about eight thousand to ten thousand different species of grasses worldwide. Bunch grasses, those that grow in clumps, cover much of the savannas.

Grasses are typically defined by height. On the Serengeti, dropseed is a common short grass, one that grows to be about 20 inches (50 cm) or less. Red oat is a common mid-height grass that grows to be between 20 and 59 inches (50 and 150 cm). Hyperthelia is an example of a tall Serengeti grass, reaching a height of 59 inches (150 cm) or more.

The Upside-Down Tree

Grasses aren't the only hardy plants that live in this region. Several trees have developed special strategies for survival in the savanna. Fire-resistant palms grow throughout Emas National Park in Brazil's cerrado region.

Baobab trees found in Africa and Australia are basically living water towers. Their soft trunks swell to allow the trees to store water—as much as 2,377 gallons at a time (9,000 liters). Natives of Africa call the baobab an upside-down tree because it looks as though its roots are in the air. The tree has a swollen trunk, stunted branches, and a wide root system. These **deciduous** trees, ones that shed their leaves annually, range in height from 16 to 98 feet (5 to 30 m) and can live several thousand years.

The baobab tree produces only tiny fingerlike clusters of leaves during the wet season. The leaves' small size helps limit water loss.

Better than Gold

Acacias are the most common trees found in the tropical grasslands. These thorny members of the pea family grow to be about 33 feet (10 m) tall and have distinctive flat tops.

Everyone loves acacia trees—at least if they live on the savanna. In Africa, giraffes feed on the leaves of the tallest part

A giraffe's long tongue can wrap around an acacia branch and pluck off leaves while avoiding thorns. Because of the giraffes' height, these animals encounter little competition for their preferred food.

The thorns of acacias don't bother olive baboons, which feed on the trees' seedpods. The olive baboon, Africa's most common baboon, is the largest of all the monkeys.

Ants establish colonies in the thorns of some acacia species. These ants feed on the tree's nectar and in return, the ants attack any insect or mammal that tries to eat the tree. However, the ants don't affect this Patas monkey. On the contrary, he climbs the acacia looking for ants to eat. Patas monkeys are the world's fastest terrestrial primates— running at speeds of 35 miles per hour (56 kilometers per hour).

of the tree. Gerenuks, a type of antelope, stand on their hind legs to reach the lowest portion of the trees. The smallest antelope in the world, the dik-dik, which stands only 14 to 16 inches (35 to 40 cm) at the shoulder, will feed on whatever leaves it can reach. Baboons eat the trees' seedpods. Weaverbirds build their nests in the branches.

Savanna termites are the architects of the creature world. The world's tallest non-human structures are built by these macro-termites. If a human being were the size of an average termite, the relative size of a single termite mound is the equivalent of a 180-story building—almost 2000 feet high

Chapter Three

Landscapers and Gardeners

It's party time on the savanna. One night every summer, millions of winged termites take to the air to mate. They fly around for a few minutes, land, pair off, mate, and then dig a new colony.

Termites aren't the only ones celebrating this night. "The sky is black with thousands of black kites [birds] coming in to feast on the termites," says Scott

Turner, an associate professor of biology at the State University of New York College of Environmental Science and Forestry. Bat-eared foxes, serval cats, and mongooses pounce on termites as they land. Hyenas, aardwolves, and aardvarks lick them up off the ground in heaps. The local people gather them up and fry them on coals or hot skillets.

Insects are the backbone of any biome. Not only are they next in the food chain after plants, but they are also the workers—breaking up soil, pollinating the flowers, and tending to the landscaping by consuming dead plant and animal matter. This is especially true of the *Macrotermitinae* termites that live in the tropical grassland region.

Most termites don't fly or breed. Alates are termites that can do both. Each year they swarm and establish new termite mounds. The alates become the king and queen of the colony. On average, the queen lays one egg every three seconds.

Everyone Loves Termites

Anteaters, armadillos, aardwolves, aardvarks, and bat-eared foxes eat termites all year round. Ground squirrels, mongooses, and meerkats live in abandoned termite mounds and

A Nice Place to Live

Some species of savanna termites build nests or mounds up to 20 feet (6 m) tall out of sun-baked mud, using their saliva and excrement to bind the soil. There are more termite mounds on the Brazilian plains than anywhere else in the world.

leopards and cheetahs use the mounds as lookouts. Monitor lizards dig into termite nests to lay eggs. Elephants use termite mounds as scratching posts. But even more important, termites replenish the soil by returning nutrients to the environment.

A group of beisa oryx eats soil at an abandoned termite mound.

In My Garden

Herbivores such as these flying termites feed on **cellulose**, a chain of sugar molecules found in plant material. Many animals, such as humans and carnivores, can't break this chain. Even termites can't digest cellulose directly. These innovative insects break the chain by growing fungi similar to mold in special fungus gardens in their mounds. They gather dead plant material outside the mound, such as wood, grass, and

Termite mounds contain up to 60 tons of soil materials per hectare (2.5 acres).

other flowering plants, and feed it to the fungi within, which break down the cellulose. The termites come along later and eat the products of this breakdown. The fungus garden is essentially an accessory stomach and intestine for the termite colony.

Giving Back to the Environment

After the dead plant material is decomposed in the fungus garden and the termites have eaten what they need, the waste is churned into the soil of the nest. During general upkeep, termites carry a lot of this soil to the surface of the mound, where it washes into the ground. This soil is filled with nutrients that help nourish the land.

An Extra Stomach

Instead of fungus gardens, some herbivores, such as gazelles, wildebeests, and giraffes, have a large sac or an additional stomach called a **rumen** where special bacteria ferment the grass. After eating, these grass-eaters, called **ruminants**, rest and rechew the cud, or partly digested grass. This helps them digest the cellulose.

Rhinoceroses, zebras, and elephants have a different approach to digestion. They ferment grass inside a pouch in their intestines. These animals feed on grasses that are not very nutritious. To compensate, they eat rapidly and consume a lot of food. An elephant spends three-quarters of its day eating. If it also had to chew cud, it would have no time for sleep.

Cleanup Crew

Dung beetles are the janitors of the savanna. They clean up the grassland by eating dung or animal droppings. Female beetles also use the dung during reproduction. They shape the dung into 1- or 2-inch (2.5- or 5-cm) balls. After burying the ball, the female will lay a single egg inside it. Some of the dung's nutrients serve as food for the beetle's larva, and the remainder is available to the soil as fertilizer. This cleanup crew reduces the spread of disease-causing parasites and microbes that thrive in the warm atmosphere of dung.

The ancient Egyptians revered dung beetles, also known as scarabs, as a symbol of renewed life.

More than forty different species of hoofed mammals live on the Serengeti Plain. Huge herds of hoofed mammals used to live on the open plains of most of the world's grasslands. Today, few large herds remain, except in Africa.

Chapter Four

Hoofed Vegetarians

It's January on the Serengeti. Hundreds of thousands of wildebeests and zebras march as if in a parade. An endless sea of legs and bodies moves steadily southward. These animals are migrating. Instead of relocating to warmer regions as many birds do in the United States, these animals follow the rain.

Every year, more than a million and half wildebeests and a quarter of a million zebras make the 500-to 700-mile (800- to 1,100-km) trek from north of the

Mara River southward to the Serengeti Plain and back again. They migrate in a circular pattern, like the hands of a clock, following the same route that has been used for centuries.

Why the wildebeests migrate to begin with is still a mystery. There is grass all year round north of the Mara River. So why leave? One theory suggests that the grass contains very little phosphorus, a mineral that is necessary for healthy bones. While grazing in the Mara River area during the dry season, the wildebeests develop a phosphorus deficiency. The deficiency disappears when the wildebeests return to eating the mineral-rich grass of the Serengeti Plain in the rainy season.

Why the wildebeests migrate is still a mystery. One theory suggests the move might be based on the need for phosphorus: a mineral that is necessary for healthy bones.

Don't Like to Travel

Wildebeests and zebras are migratory **grazers**, or grass eaters that move from place to place. They share the savanna with resident, or non-migratory, grazers, such as the topi and kongoni antelope.

Topi are reddish-colored antelopes with blue legs. They weigh about 220 pounds (100 kilograms). Kongoni are light brown antelopes, weighing about 275 pounds (125 kg). Their long, slim muzzles allow them to reach down within the grass to pluck the tender, nutritious parts of the grass plants. Resident grazers do not roam over large geographic areas. Instead, they occupy home ranges.

Grazers also share the savanna with non-migratory and migratory **browsers**, mammals that eat tree and shrub leaves and berries as well as grass. These include giraffes and elephants.

Giraffes don't migrate. The giraffe is the world's tallest land mammal, reaching heights of up to 20 feet (6 m). Its

Giraffes have the same number of bones in their neck as you do. However, elongated vertebrae make their neck longer.

neck alone is about 7 feet long (2.2 m). Even though giraffes look tall and skinny, they are not lightweight. One giraffe can weigh as much as 2,800 pounds (1,270 kg). But then, nothing about giraffes is small. Giraffes' tongues are about 18 inches (45 cm) long.

Elephants are migratory browsers. During the dry season, the animals travel in a giant circle and follow wetlands and lakes. Elephants are the largest living land animals, weighing up to 16,500 pounds (7,500 kg). Unlike humans, elephants never stop growing. Their body size continues to increase through life, so the largest elephant in a group is likely also to be the oldest. If you see a herd of elephants, you are probably looking at females, as adult bull elephants are loners. The oldest female is considered the leader.

Share and Share Alike

Up to sixteen species of hoofed mammals, or **ungulates**, may coexist in the same area. They share not only the same land but also the same plants, each eating a slightly different part.

Zebras are the only grazers with upper as well as lower incisors, or cutting teeth. They feed on the tops of tough red oat and star grass plants. This clears the way for the wildebeests to eat the tender middle leaves and stems. The gazelles then enjoy the new shoots.

Safety in Numbers

Life on a grassland isn't just about eating—it's also about not being eaten. Herbivores have evolved special adaptations for survival, such as good eyesight, fighting techniques, speed, or unusual running patterns that give them some advantage over carnivores. But perhaps their best defense is living in herds. The risk of being hunted is smaller when you are one of hundreds than when you are on your own. First, there are more eyes and ears watching for danger. What may look like a friendly gesture between two zebras, in which one stands with its head resting on another's back, actually provides the zebras with a 360-degree view of the surrounding area.

Camouflage is also more effective in a herd. Zebras may not appear to be camouflaged, with their black and white stripes set against the brown grasslands. But lions and leopards don't see in color; they see shapes. The vertical pattern of the zebra's stripes makes it almost impossible for a predator to distinguish one individual from another.

Finally, when a predator does attack, it focuses on a single animal. When a lion charges at a herd of antelopes, the animals scatter in all directions. This leaves the lion disoriented, which sometimes gives the antelopes enough time to escape.

Other Herbivores of the Savanna

The savannas of Africa, South America, and Australia have similar climates, soil, and topography, yet each continent has evolved its own unique animal community. Neither South

America nor Australia has Africa's large herds of herbivores. The llanos in South America can lay claim, however, to the world's largest rodent, the capybara. Also called the water pig or water cavy, the capybara resembles a huge guinea pig. It rarely strays from water and eats aquatic plants and grass. The rodent may grow to be 50 inches (130 cm) in length and weigh up to 175 pounds (80 kg). People hunt capybaras for their meat, which is salted, dried, and eaten, especially during Easter. Their skin is used to make leather.

A capybaras' hard teeth can easily cut through the toughest grasses and water reed.

What's in the Pocket?

Africa, Asia, and the Americas share similar species of mammals. Scientists believe that these similarities exist because all the continents were joined together at one time and animals freely migrated from one landmass to the other. Australia however, is home to animals not seen anywhere else in the world. This could be because Australia has been separate from the rest of the world for so long that its wildlife population had no influence from the outside until people began introducing animals to it from other continents.

Dry as a Bone

Australia is the world's driest continent.

One of Australia's most famous grassland animals is the kangaroo. The young kangaroo is born at an early stage of development and must crawl through its mother's fur to her pouch, where it stays until it is about six months of age. This marsupial is not a picky eater. It can grow fat by eating the poorest-quality grass on the driest grassland.

Kangaroos range in size from less than 1 foot (30 cm) to more than 7 feet (2.2 m) tall. Only the larger kangaroos, the red kangaroo and the Eastern and Western grey kangaroo, inhabit grassland. With their powerful hind legs, they can bound across the savanna at such high speeds that their only predator is man.

One-third of Australia receives an average of only 14 inches (35 cm) of rain per year, another third receives 10 inches (25 cm) or less.

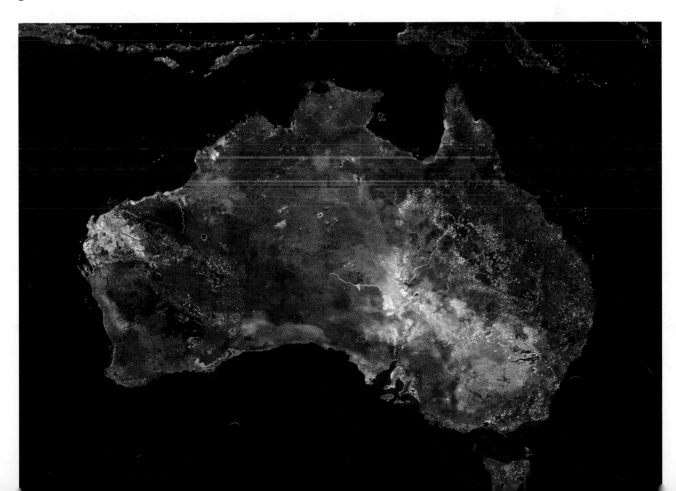

For thousands of years, royalty kept cheetahs, like this one, as hunting companions. In the 16th century, emperors of India used trained cheetahs to bring down antelopes. Today, cheetahs are extinct in India. Only small populations live in the Middle East and Africa.

Chapter Five

Tooth and Claw

Where there are herbivores, there will be carnivores. These predators help keep herds of herbivores healthy by eliminating the weak and sickly so that only the strongest animals are left to reproduce. Carnivores also preserve the ecosystem by keeping the number of prey down to a population that the environment can support.

On the Serengeti, there is approximately one predatory animal for every one hundred prey animals. As herbivores have different preferences for food, so do carnivores. Each is equipped with its own technique for hunting its favorite game.

The cheetah depends on speed. It is the fastest animal on earth, reaching speeds of 70 miles per hour (110 kph). It can't sustain that pace for long, however—only for about 300 yards (275 m), or the length of three football fields. For this reason, its hunt is not always successful. The cheetah's favorite prey, the antelope, often zigzags and escapes.

At one time, cheetahs lived in the grasslands of Africa, Asia, Europe, and North America. About ten thousand years ago, climate changes caused all but one species of the cheetah to become extinct. With such drastic reductions in their numbers, close relatives were forced to mate, and the cheetah became genetically inbred. This means that all cheetahs are closely related. If everyone in a population is related, there are low survival rates, poor sperm quality, and greater susceptibility to disease. This could eventually lead to the animal's extinction. Scientists are working on ways to help the cheetah survive through natural and artificial breeding programs.

Don't Mess with Me

Then there is the king of the beasts, with its bushy, flowing mane and "don't mess with me" attitude. Lions can take down a wildebeest or zebra with just one bite. However, lions are lazy. A typical lion is active for only one to seven hours each day. The rest of its time is spent sleeping or lying around in the shade.

Cat Trouble

Of the thirty-six species of cats in the world, such as lions, cheetahs, and leopards, most are threatened or endangered, with one exception—the domestic feline.

Although males can and do hunt, females are the primary breadwinners and usually hunt in groups. Lions cannot run quickly. They manage about 40 miles per hour (65 kph), but their prey runs faster. Instead, lions depend on stealth. Females don't have manes, so it is easier for them to sneak up on a herd of herbivores. Lions also depend on their ability to jump. From a standing position, a lion can jump up to 12 feet (3.5 m) high or cover a distance of 40 feet (12 m).

Lions are the only truly sociable member of the cat family. They live in family groups called prides.

A Bad Reputation

For a long time, scientists thought hyenas were only scavengers because these animals were often seen lying around and waiting for a lion to finish eating before they ate. But then researchers discovered that it is the lion that chases hyenas away from their own kills. Hyenas are in fact expert hunters. A single hyena can catch an adult wildebeest that weighs up to 380 pounds (170 kg) after chasing it for 3 miles (5 km) at speeds of up to 37 miles per hour (60 kph).

Hyenas are known for their voracious eating habits as well as eating in packs. A group of 38 spotted hyenas have been seen to dismember a zebra in 15 minutes.

Hyenas are master scavengers as well. Thanks to a hearty digestive system, they can consume and digest parts of a kill that other mammals leave untouched.

Carnivore of the Smaller Variety

The zorilla, or striped polecat, of Africa resembles the American striped skunk. It even reacts to danger by ejecting a foul-smelling fluid from its anal glands. This fluid is more potent than the American variety. It aims straight for its attacker's face and can cause temporary blindness in its victim. The smell is

The name zorilla *is a derivation of the Spanish word* zorro, *which means "fox."*

so bad that people of the Sudan nicknamed the zorilla the "father of stinks."

Apparently, the zorilla is well respected by larger carnivores. According to the International Wildlife Encyclopedia, one zorilla once held nine adult lions at bay while it nibbled on their freshly killed zebra carcass.

Carnivores of the Llanos

Africa may have the largest, fastest, and most ferocious land mammals, but South America has its share of giants as well. The giant anteater is a termite colony's worst enemy. It rips open a termite hill with its clawed feet. Then the anteater works its 24-inch (60-cm)-long tongue into the heart of the colony. Insects stick to the tongue as if it were flypaper. One giant anteater can eat up to thirty thousand termites in a single day. The giant anteater of South America, about the size of a German shepherd dog, is covered with stiff, strawlike hair that grows up to 16 inches (40 cm) long on the tail.

The anteater's principal enemies are pumas, jaguars, and humans. Giant anteaters are hunted for trophies, for meat, and because they are mistakenly believed to kill dogs and cattle.

Long Legs

The maned wolf of South America is the second-largest member of the dog family. Only the gray wolf is larger. It gets its name from the mane of long, dark hair on the back of its neck and shoulders. It is a solitary, nocturnal animal that hunts small rodents, such as mice, but sometimes eats fruits and sugarcane.

Farmers often kill the maned wolf because they mistakenly believe the animal is a threat to their livestock. Because of its long legs, it could possibly outrun its attackers, but the animal doesn't even try. It has no natural predators except humans, so it has no concept of the need for flight. Many fear that this animal will soon become extinct.

None of Its Own

Australia is the only place in the world that can claim no large predators of its own. The closest thing to a "big" carnivore in Australia is the dingo—the wild dog. Ironically, the dingo is a descendant of domesticated dogs brought to Australia thousands of years ago by the Aborigines. Dingoes eat small mammals and insects. Today, dingoes have interbred with domestic dogs, and the two are physically indistinguishable. In fact, there may be only a few purebred dingoes alive today.

Let's Dig

Burrowers are the cultivators of the grassland, helping break up and aerate the soil by digging. These include the smaller grassland animals, such as mice and rats.

Perhaps one of the most famous burrowers of South America is the armadillo. Armadillos are shy, and information about their biology remains largely anecdotal, though many local people can tell you how to fry, boil, or marinate them. The

word *armadillo* is Spanish for one that is armed. Its shell, called a **carapace**, is made up of small plates of bone.

Although it looks like armor, the carapace is not always an effective shield against enemies. In the case of the nine-banded armadillo, the shell is only 0.1 inch (2 mm) thick, and even dogs can bite through it. However, the carapace does provide protection against the thorny undergrowth where the armadillo hides from trouble and forages for food.

Out of twenty species, the giant armadillo is the most rare. It can grow up to 3 feet (90 cm) in length and weigh up to 122 pounds (55 kg). It feeds primarily on ants and termites.

Local tribes use the carapace of the giant armadillo as a cradle or boat. Charangos, or traditional stringed instruments, are made from the carapaces of the smaller species.

The Local Garbage Truck

With all these predators, there is bound to be a mess of dead animals. Call in the cleanup crew: vultures. Vultures are scavengers—the garbage trucks for grasslands all over the world—eating dead animals, or **carrion**, which would otherwise attract insects and act as a breeding ground for diseases.

Lions and hyenas frequently follow vultures to find a kill.

A vulture's nearly naked head, neck, legs, and feet are an advantage for a bird that regularly thrusts its head into rotting carcasses. A lack of feathers makes these areas easier to clean, which prevents bacterial and fungal growth. Because their bills cannot break through animal skin, vultures must wait for a carcass to decompose or for another animal to attack it before they can feed.

Not Picky Eaters

Birds have had to develop their own special adaptations to the tropical grassland biome. Birds that are strictly herbivores are scarce because fruit is in short supply in the savanna. Therefore, the majority of birds in tropical grassland are omnivores. Because there are so few trees, grassland birds build nests on the ground. This makes their eggs and young extremely vulnerable to predators and trampling. To compensate for the danger, most chicks leave the nest as soon as they are able to walk.

The ostrich is the largest living bird in the world. A male may stand more than 9 feet (2.7 m) tall. With its long legs, an adult can run up to 44 miles per hour (70 kph).

Two other flightless, long-legged birds resemble the ostrich in looks and lifestyle, though they are not closely related. The emu lives in Australia, and the rhea lives in South America. Scientists believe the similarities among the ostrich, emu, and rhea are due to **convergent evolution**. This occurs when unrelated animals develop similar physical features and lifestyles because they had to adapt to similar environmental conditions.

An Oxpecker on My Shoulder

Some birds enjoy the company of mammals and will use them to their benefit. Water buffalos, rhinoceroses, sable antelopes, and hippopotamuses often have oxpeckers, also called tickbirds, riding on their backs. The oxpecker eats ticks and other parasites from its host's skin. The bird consumes a good meal, while cleaning the animal's hide. The birds also alert their hosts to the presence of predators. This partnership is an example of **mutualism**—a relationship between two species that benefits both. An oxpecker comes equipped with special curved and sharp claws that allow it to clutch the hide of its animal—even if the host is galloping at full speed.

A Fulbe-Waila nomadic community moves to greener pastures, just as their ancestors have done for hundreds of years.

Chapter Six

People and the Grasslands

The animals and plants of the tropical grasslands are affected every day by human activity. Farmers, industrialists, hunters, poachers, and tourists all leave their mark, and their numbers have grown over time.

For thousands of years, **nomadic** tribes, such as the Fulani and Masai, raised cattle, goats, and sheep on the African savanna. They moved with their domesticated herds in a constant search for water and greener pastures. Today, these tribes have settled in villages. More permanent settlement allows children to attend school and families to get better health care. But the animals these people raise are now confined by fences to much smaller areas for grazing.

Cattle, goats, and sheep are heavy grazers, meaning they crop plants down to the ground. Instead of eating a fraction of the plant life before moving on to other areas, as they did when they moved around, the animals now consume everything on their farmland.

With no vegetation to anchor it, topsoil blows away. This erosion turns grassland into desert. Nothing is able to grow back, even during the rainy season. This situation, called desertification, benefits no one. Vast areas of Africa, Australia, and India have already turned from grassland into desert.

Sustainable Development

During the last thirty years or so, many people have come to understand the importance of conserving tropical grasslands for people and for animals. Environmental organizations work with local businesspeople and farmers to promote a healthy relationship with their environment. This is called sustainable economic development.

In 2003, at the African Wildlife Foundation "Conservation is Good Business" symposium in Washington, D.C., the pres-

Water, Please

Confining cattle, sheep, and goats with fencing causes more damage than just overgrazing. Fences also restrict the movements of wild animals. In many cases, fences prevent wildebeests from reaching familiar watering holes and feeding areas that have been used for years. As a result, more wildebeests are dying of thirst than ever before.

ident of Botswana, Festus Mogae, embraced the concept of sustainable economic development as the only option that offers hope for struggling African countries.

For many countries like Botswana, which are heavily dependent on wildlife, tourism, and agriculture, sustainable economic development has become synonymous with a way to create jobs and revenue without destroying the environment.

Helping Hands

Local residents in South America and Africa are taking active roles in developing sustainable farming practices. The Waterberg Conservancy, a private group of landowners in Namibia, agrees to stock ranches with fewer cattle and remove fences between adjacent parcels of land. This gives wild animals wider ranges in which to roam, and desertification decreases. Furthermore, private landowners and tourism boards can make money and thus help the economy of these struggling countries by offering big-game hunting. "Today, people feel like they have a real stake in the conservation of their country, and it is becoming economically important to conserve," says Scott Turner.

New Problem

Poaching, or illegal hunting, is still a problem. Over the years, Sam McNaughton, a Syracuse University biology professor, has seen the black rhinoceros and elephant populations almost completely disappear from the Serengeti because of

Although it has been outlawed, poaching of elephants for their tusks is still practiced in many African countries.

illegal hunting. In China, rhinoceros horns are used as medicine and are in huge demand.

Today, there are international laws regulating the trade of rhinoceros horns and elephant tusk ivory. Although they are still hunted, elephants, at least, appear to be making a comeback. Another type of hunting has expanded in recent years—meat poaching. This is big business, says McNaughton. Locals are killing resident grazers, such as gazelles and topi, and shipping the meat to local markets. "Many Africans are poor," McNaughton says. "Meat poachers say they can make more money from poaching than they can from doing anything else."

Vacation Time

Perhaps the best promoter for conservation has been the increase in tourism, which provides local people with an alternative source of income.

Until a few decades ago, cattle grazing was the main economic base of the Australian savannas. Tourism now brings in more income than does the cattle industry.

"In South Africa, conservationists were able to get the message across that the white rhino is important to save because it brings in dollars from tourists," says Terry Wolf, wildlife director at Lion Country Safari near West Palm Beach in Florida. "If there are no rhinos, there will be no tourists."

To protect the animals, the South African government hired poachers to act as rhinoceros bodyguards. Each man was assigned to one animal and told to follow it around all day, every day. "Who better to protect an animal from a poacher than an ex-poacher who knows all the tricks?" says Wolf.

Tourism plays a critical economic role for the protection of the animals, habitat, and life on the savanna.

A Little Help from Zoos

Zoos are also getting into the act of conservation. The American Zoo and Aquarium Association sponsors the Species Survival Plan (SSP). The SSP is a captive-animal management program for threatened animals. Animals in the SSP get special attention from biologists who educate the public about environmental threats and work with government organizations and biologists in the countries where the species live to initiate conservation programs.

The bongo, an antelope native to Kenya, has not been seen in that country for many years. Thanks to the SSP, the bongo was reintroduced to the country in 2004.

What You Can Do

Tropical grasslands are wonderful, fragile places. Just as each aspect of the biome depends on another, these areas also depend on people to understand and protect them. That's where you come in. You may not live on a savanna. Most Africans don't, either. But everyone can help protect these places through educating others about their importance. You can also get involved with any number of organizations that are working to protect tropical grasslands. Local zoos and aquariums often have education and volunteer projects for which they need helping hands. The American Zoo and Aquarium Association has many other ideas about how you can get involved with conservation efforts on their Web site www.azasweb.com/kids.

Glossary

basal meristem—growing point of the grass plant, located at the base of the stem

biome—community of living organisms in a single ecological region

browser—animal that eats grasses, tree and shrub leaves, and berries

campo—tropical grassland in South America south of the Amazon Rain Forest, lying primarily in Brazil

carapace—hard, bony outer covering, such as an armadillo's shell

carnivore—animal that eats only meat

carrion—dead animal

cellulose—main constituent of plant tissues and fibers; composed of tough strings of sugar molecules

controlled burn—fire that people set and manage to ensure that only a certain area of land is burned

convergent evolution—process by which unrelated animals living in different parts of the world evolve similar physical traits because they had to adapt to similar environmental conditions

cyanobacterium—microorganism that fixes, or pulls, nitrogen from the air, making it available to plants

deciduous—kind of tree that sheds its leaves annually

decomposer—organism that breaks down dead organic matter into its component parts

diversity—number of different species of plants or animals living in a given area

edaphic savanna—tropical grassland created because of poor soil conditions that cannot support tree growth

enzyme—protein produced by living organisms that speeds up chemical reactions

grazer—animal that eats only grass

herbivore—animal that eats only plants

impermeable—not penetrable

Intertropical Convergence Zone—region that circles Earth near the equator, where the trade winds of the northern and southern hemispheres meet

litter—dead plants that make up the uppermost layer of soil and contain valuable nutrients needed for new plants to grow

llano—tropical grassland in South America north of the Amazon Rain Forest, found primarily in Venezuela

marsupial—animal that carries its young in a pocket, such as the kangaroo, wallaby, and wombat

mutualism—relationship between two organisms that benefits both partners

nomadic—roaming from place to place without having a permanent home

omnivore—animal that eats both meat and plants

photosynthesis—process through which green plants use sunlight to form sugars

producer—organism such as a plant that produces its own food

rumen—in grazing animals, an additional stomach in which grass is stored and fermented by microbes

ruminant—animal that must rechew its food after it has fermented in the rumen

transpiration—evaporation of water from a plant's leaves

ungulate—hoofed mammalian herbivore

To Find Out More

Books

Allaby, Michael. *Tropical Grasslands*. Vol. 9, *Biomes of the World*. Danbury, Conn.: Grolier Educational, 1999.

Bash, Barbara. *Tree of Life: The World of the African Baobab*. Gibbs Smith, 2002.

Beani, Laura, and Dessi Francesco. *World Nature Encyclopedia: African Savanna*. Austin, Tex.: Raintree Steck-Vaughn Publishers, 1989.

Horton, Catherine. *A Closer Look at Grasslands*. New York and Toronto: Penguin Books Ltd., 1979.

Knapp, Brian. *What Do We Know About Grasslands?* New York: Peter Bedrick Books, 1992.

Morgan, Ben. *Biomes Atlases: Tropical Grasslands*. Austin, Tex.: Raintree Steck-Vaughn Publishers, 2003.

Planet Earth: Grasslands and Tundra. Alexandria, Va.: Time-Life Books Inc., 1985.

Silver, Donald M. *One Small Square: African Savanna*. New York: W.H. Freeman and Company, 1994.

Taylor, Dave. *The Lion and the Savannah*. New York: Crabtree Publishing Company, 1990.

Taylor, Dave. *Endangered Savannah Animals*. New York: Crabtree Publishing Company, 1992.

Videos

The Living Planet, Episode 5: Seas of Grass. The John D. & Catherine T. MacArthur Foundation; Library Video Classics Project, British Broadcasting Corporation/Time-Life Video, 1984.

DVDs

Africa: The Serengeti. SlingShot Entertainment, Burbank, Calif.: 2001.

Organizations and Online Sites

The Australian Government's Cooperative Research Centres Program on Tropical Savannas
http://savanna.cdu.edu.au

African Wildlife Resources
http://www.africanwildliferesources.org
This site has links to sources and environmental organizations involved with tropical grasslands.

African Wildlife Foundation
1400 Sixteenth Street NW, Suite 120
Washington, DC 20036
Phone: 202-939-3333
Fax: 202-939-3332
e-mail: africanwildlife@awf.org
www.awf.org

American Zoo and Aquarium Association
8403 Colesville Road, Suite 710
Silver Spring, MD 20910-3314
Phone: 301-562-0777
Fax: 301-562-0888
www.aza.org

A Note on Sources

A writing teacher once told me that you know you've done enough research when you pick up on contradictions in the sources you are using. She was right. Science is a field that constantly evolves. New research and techniques often disprove old theories. When researching this book, I read countless books, magazine and newspaper articles, and Web pages. Instead of relying on the material I read, I contacted the authors directly, such as Samuel McNaughton from Syracuse University and Scott Turner from the State University of New York College of Environmental Science and Forestry. This led to several helpful interviews and a wealth of additional information. Although I could not visit the tropical grasslands in person, I did visit the Denver Zoo so that I could see the animals I was writing about. I also contacted the American Zoo and Aquarium Association, the World Wildlife Fund, and other conservation groups to find out what was currently being done to help preserve the grasslands.   —*Laurie Peach Toupin*

Index

Numbers in *italics* indicate illustrations.

About the Author

Laurie Peach Toupin loves nature and enjoys helping others uncover its mysteries through writing and teaching. She's an environmental instructor with River Classroom, a hands-on freshwater school program. She also led an environmental after-school program called the Monoosnoc Brook Patrol for middle schools in Leominster, Massachusetts.

She has an undergraduate degree in environmental engineering from the University of Pittsburgh. While getting her master's degree in journalism from the University of Missouri, Laurie worked at the Missouri Department of Conservation. Today, she is a freelance writer of children's books.

In her free time, Laurie enjoys hiking, canoeing, and camping with her husband, their two daughters, and their two dogs.

Laurie has always longed to visit Australia and Africa. Thanks to this book, she has had the opportunity to visit them through writing.